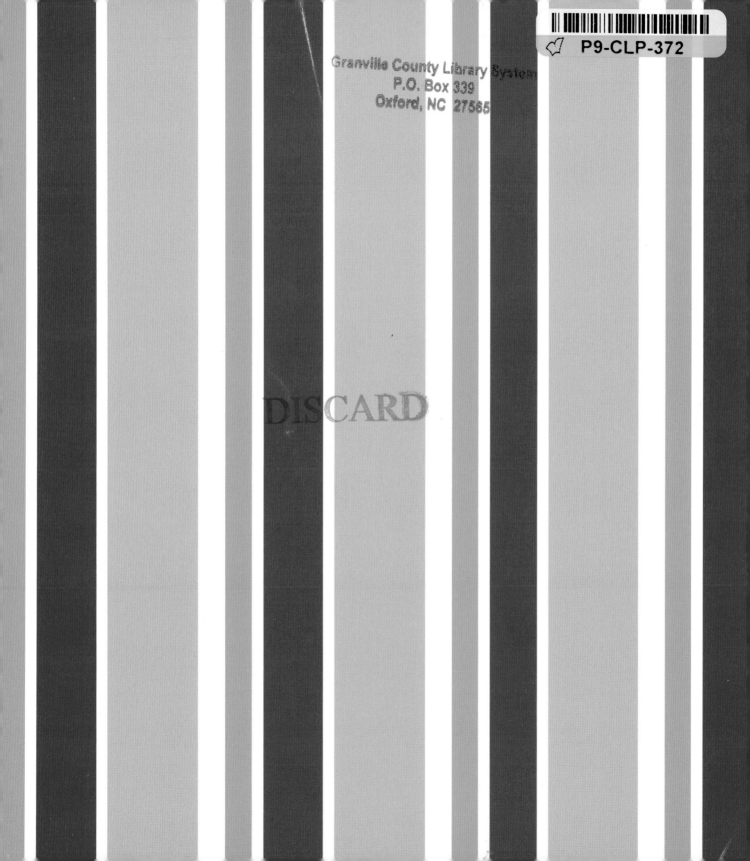

P9-CLP-372

When Everybody Wore a Hat Copyright © 2003 by William Steig Manufactured in China. All rights reserved. www.harperchildrens.com
Library of Congress Cataloging-in-Publication Data Steig, William. When everybody wore a hat / William Steig.—1st ed. p. cm.
ISBN 0-06-009700-0 — ISBN 0-06-009701-9 (lib. bdg.) 1. Steig, William, 1907– —Homes and haunts—New York (State)—New York.
2. Bronx (New York, N.Y.)—Social life and customs. 3. Steig, William, 1907– —Childhood and youth. 4. Authors, American—
20th century—Biography. 5. Illustrators—United States—Biography. 6. Cartoonists—United States—Biography.
7. Bronx (New York, N.Y.)—Biography. I. Title. PS3537.T3178 Z478 2003 813'.54—dc21 2002006512
Typography by Alicia Mikles 1 2 3 4 5 6 7 8 9 10 ❖ First Edition

When Everybody Wore a Hat

WILLIAM STEIG

JOANNA COTLER BOOKS
An Imprint of HarperCollins*Publishers*

In 1916, when I was eight years old, there were almost no electric lights, cars or telephones—and definitely no TV. Even fire engines were pulled by horses. Kids went to LIBRARIES for books. There were lots of immigrants.

This is me climbing a tree in the Bronx, where I spent most of my childhood.

Mom and Pop came to America from the Old Country. This is my family at the supper table. I was the second youngest.

We all lived in a small apartment. It was impossible to be alone.

Sometimes Mom and Pop quarreled.

They spoke four languages: German, Polish, Yiddish and English. They spoke Polish a lot. Who knows what they were saying? But we learned the important words.

When there wasn't enough heat, Pop even fought with the radiator.

My father and mother went to the opera pretty often. Caruso was Pop's favorite singer. He would listen to his records on our phonograph. You had to wind it up with a handle.

Pop loved to play chess with Mr. Hoffman. He said that Mr. Hoffman was the most intelligent man he had ever met.

This was Mom's best friend. In those days, women wore corsets and heels and hats—sometimes with fruit. There was no such thing as a hatless human being. Cops had hats. Criminals had hats. Even monkeys.

There were times when sad news would come from the Old Country. It made us scared to see Mom cry.

Pop was an expert rower.

The prettiest girl on the block was Marian Mack. Back then boys never played with girls.

Mom said Esther Haberman had a big mouth.

For a nickel you could get a lot: a hot dog sandwich from a stand. A pound of fruit. A movie. And two movies if you sat in the same seat. A movie was even called a "Nickelette."

A nickel was money.

On your birthday you might get a nickel.

We moved a lot. The moving men were very strong.

We used to go shopping with Mom all the time. We went along to carry stuff. This is Barney, our butcher.

Rich people from Europe wore different clothes.
And hats. Remember what I said about hats?

Even though it was on the other side of the world,
we all knew there was a big war going on in Europe. It
was World War I.

Prince was the janitor's dog. Kids were scared of him.

This lady lived in the corner building. She had lots of cats.

Mrs. Kingman always had a dog. That was unusual. She used to pass through our neighborhood all the time, but she was too elegant to live there. She was looked on by the women with admiration.

We never went to a doctor's office, or even a hospital. Our doctor's name was Dr. Wager, and he came to our house. I wasn't afraid of the doctor, but my brothers were.

Dr. Wager had to visit my brother Henry a few times.
Once he had Spanish influenza.

I got my first haircut at Ditchick's Barbershop, which was across the street from my building on Brooke Avenue. I got to listen to all kinds of stories.

Everyone wanted his picture on a horse. To be sitting on a horse like a cowboy was really something.

Cameras were very big then, and you had to stay very still. This was hard for the horse.

In 1916, when everybody wore a hat, I was eight years old. When I grew up, I wanted to be an artist or a seaman.

And this is a picture of me today, without a
hat. I did become an artist, but not a seaman.

William Steig